HOW TO ARGUE

WITH YOUR SPOUSE

Ron Dentinger ◆ Rich Renik ◆ Chuck Gekas

DEDICATION

Just as a magnifying glass enlarges things so they are easier to see and understand, so too the exaggerations used in humor enlarge our faults and our frailties. As a result they become easier to see, to understand and, more important, to manage.

To paraphrase an old saying:

> "Humor is like the springs on a wagon.
> It smooths out the bumps in the road."

The authors and their wives firmly believe in family values, and dedicate this book to all those couples who care enough to make their marriages work.

TABLE OF CONTENTS

Introduction 1

The Stealth Attack 3

Using Body Language 3

Using the Sympathetic Advantage 3

The Need To Start Slowly 13

Extreme Actions And Reactions 23

The Psychological Edge 25

The Grass Is Greener 27

The Compromise Gambit 29

The Need For Preparation 31

Saving Face 35

Summary 39

About The Authors 41

Here's a great line that plays on your spouse's sympathy.
You say:

"I want to thank you for accepting all my faults . . .
. . . and for pointing them out in the first place."

◆ ◆ ◆

If your spouse continues to point out your faults, say:

"The way you find fault, you'd think there was a reward."

OR

Pretend to have hurt feelings with:

"I hate my faults too, because they are the very things
that kept me from marrying somebody better than you."

◆ ◆ ◆

On the other hand,
if you need to point out some of your spouse's faults,
you can do so . . . just refer to your comments as:

"Constructive criticism."

If your spouse says:

"Getting married is like eating in a restaurant.
About the time you get what you asked for,
you notice what somebody else has,
and you kind of wish that you would have had that."

or, if your spouse says:

"Marriage is a lot like a midnight phone call.
First there's a ring, and then you wake up."

You can say:

"Well, I can remember when and where I got married,
but I'll be damned if I can remember why."

START SLOWLY

If you're commenting on your spouse's weight during breakfast
use a softer, gentler approach. Like:

"You're everything I ever wanted and more.
About 50 pounds more."

At night, however, anything goes.
When your spouse says:

"Will you please get up and close the curtains?
I don't want the neighbors to see me in my underwear."

You can say:

"If the neighbors see you in your underwear,
THEY will close **THEIR** curtains."

OR

When your spouse goes to the kitchen for a snack,
you can say:

"If you gain any more weight,
I think you might qualify for some money
from the **SAVE THE WHALE FOUNDATION.**"

MEN: If your wife makes the coffee,
on some nice sunny morning while you're eating breakfast say:

"It looks like rain."

Your wife will say: "There's not a cloud in the sky."

Then you say: "I was talking about your coffee."

WOMEN: If you are regularly ignored,
you can really get Mr. Wonderful's attention
with something like this:

While you are talking to your girlfriend on the telephone
and you are sure that your husband is listening . . .
say something like:

"Wow! You have a lot more nerve than I do.
I haven't even told my husband yet."

In any argument, both the husband and the wife can typically only see their own point of view.

Each of them claims that the other person doesn't fight fair. This will often bring about
EXTREME ACTIONS . . . AND REACTIONS.

Here is an example:

The wife is mad and immaturely locks herself in the bathroom. The far more mature husband resents her childish behavior and starts sliding things under the bathroom door.

Another example:

This time the husband is not willing to talk things out, and he takes the newspaper and goes into the bathroom. The wife will probably resent this.
In one such case the wife took extra effort to get even. She had secretly stretched Saran Wrap over the toilet bowl, and then put the seat back down.
Her reasoning was that . . . stretched tightly . . . Saran Wrap is almost invisible.

Having "**THE PSYCHOLOGICAL EDGE**" can help you
in an argument.
This is best done by getting on your spouse's nerves.
This is extremely frustrating and unsettling,
and it hinders your spouse's ability to think straight.
Let's say that you and your spouse are in a movie theater.
Do what I once did while my wife tried to watch the show.
You utter occasional comments like:

"Wow! There's a bunch of gum stuck under my seat."
(You wait a bit . . . then say:)

"There must be eight or nine pieces stuck under here."
(You wait a bit more . . . then add:)

"Yuk! This one is peppermint."

I found this to be extremely powerful.
I not only frustrated my wife;
even the people around us seemed to be somewhat unsettled.

Married couples argue before and/or after a class reunion.
On the way to your spouse's class reunion,
you might comment:

"If somebody asks me why I married you . . .
. . . what should I say?"

Cutting down your spouse's old flame
is a great way to get on the offense.

MEN: Your opening line would go something like this:

I just saw your old boyfriend, and had to wonder
if Snow White and Dopey might have had a son."

WOMEN: Your opening line might go like this:

"I heard your old girlfriend is involved in the war on drugs.
She works at the airport sniffing luggage."

These are effective because: Old flames never go out totally.
And the grass always seems greener . . .

Another powerful tool is the "**THE COMPROMISE GAMBIT.**"

You appear to be playing fair by saying something like:

"We can work it out.
If you are wrong, just admit it
and then we will forget the whole thing."

Your spouse will obviously say:

"Well, what if I'm right?"

Then you say:

"When has *THAT* ever happened?"

Another version of "**THE COMPROMISE GAMBIT**"
goes like this:

You say:

"Enough is enough.
Let's end this equitably.
If you will admit that you are wrong,
then I will admit that you are right."

If you are convincing . . . your spouse will say, "I'm wrong."
Then you say, "That's right!" and walk away.

"BEING PREPARED" is extremely important.
It is a big part of defending against surprise attacks.
Always be ready to defend your actions.

Suppose your spouse faults you for going off your diet . . .
you could modestly say:

"I guess I'm just not self-centered enough to diet.
I decided it's better to do what little I can
to help our nation's farmers."

If you forget your anniversary, your spouse will probably
question how ANYONE can forget when they got married.

If you are prepared, you can respond like this:

"I think about it a lot, but I just don't remember."

When your spouse says:

"You mean you actually can't remember
when you got married?"

You say: "Oh . . . 'when.' I thought you said, 'Why.'"

Next,
pretend to be quietly thinking
and then attempt to redeem your forgetfulness
by claiming that you don't forget everything.

You say:

"I can't forget all the things you've done . . .
no matter how hard I try."

If your spouse claims that you are a compulsive liar,

you say:

"If I lie, it's your fault. You keep asking questions."

If your spouse says: "The kids look just like me,"
you say: "Don't feel bad. At least they're healthy."

Rich Renik has been involved in music all his life. This led to a long career as an on-air radio personality in Chicago, including 13 years at WMAQ (NBC) and 12 years at US-99 (CBS). While he is still on the air, he also teaches radio at The Illinois Center for Broadcasting. (Lombard Campus)

Rich served as the host of many Muscular Dystrophy and Easter Seal Telethons on Public TV. He narrated a Christmas CD project: "Yes, Virginia, There Is A Santa Claus" backed by "The Night Before Christmas" and wrote a leadership book: "Engaging Employees in the Business of Success."

As a US Army veteran, Rich also hosts a video program for veterans which can be seen on www.VSPANN.org/channel. He is married to Barbara and resides in Orland Park, Illinois.

Read more or contact Rich via ww.RichRenik.com.

Made in the USA
San Bernardino, CA
28 March 2014